CELTIC – FOOTBALL LEGEND 1888-1938

compiled by
Stuart Marshall

© Stuart Marshall
First published in the United Kingdom, 1998
by Stenlake Publishing, Unit 16a,
Thistle Business Park North, Ayr Road,
Cumnock, Ayrshire KA18 1EQ
Telephone / fax: 01290 423114

ISBN 1 84033 043 0

The Song of the Good Old Celtic F.C.

Tune—" Wearin' o' the Green."

Och, darlin' dear, I used to cheer,
The Celts of long ago,
When Barney Battles, Divers too
Were wont to face the foe.
When Kelly, Campbell, Blessington,
Dan Doyle and all the rest,
Each Saturday upheld the truth
That Celtic were the best.
D'ye mind ould Dan MacArthur
How he used to keep the goal,
And "forward" A. MacMahon
Through the net could kick a hole
Though never a sign of any net,
In these ould days was seen,
Och, my heart it beats the warmer yet,
For the bhoys who wear the Green.

But we have just as hardy bhoys
In Celtic's Team to-day,
Although supporters all will miss
The sight of Jamie Hay.
When Sunny Jim is on the Ball
We always have to grin,
Till he passes to McMenemy,
Who parts to Jimmy Quinn.
'Tis then the goalie fails to see
The ball go whizzing by,
And then a yell is heard—"A Goal"
That seems to split the sky.
And the Celtic keep the Championship
With Parkhead for the scene,
And so here's health to the hefty Bhoys
To-day who wear the Green.

No. 2238—*Copyright.*   R. F. Morrison.

FOREWORD

I spent my formative years watching Clyde . . . but inside I longed for European football. Using the flimsy pretext that Celtic had once graced Shawfield as their home stadium, in 1963 I started slinking off to Parkhead for a bit of the exotic. There the likes of John Divers and Big Yogi Hughes dazzled and scored against teams such as FC Basle. I was at all the sixties European games. One sticks out from the rest – Red Star Belgrade, November 13th 1968, unlucky for some – but what a game wee Jimmy Johnstone had.

However, this book isn't about me or the glorious 1960s; it looks at an earlier period before the War when newspapers and comics and packets of cigarettes or sweeties gave away photos and cards of the football legends of that era. Boys badgered men at street corners with the plea 'Got any fag cards, mister?'. Now grown men, like me, who have been collecting this stuff for twenty years or more pay sometimes large sums of money for the give-aways of yesteryear. Why do we do this? Because we're Celtic fans!

PS Sorry, Clyde.

The 1888 team:
Back row: Committee men J McDonald, J Glass, D Malloy, J J Quillan, Joe Anderson (Trainer)
Middle row: M Dunbar, W Maley, W Dunning, W McKillop (Committee), P Gallacher, John O'Hara (Committee), T E Maley, W Groves
Front row: M McKeown, N McCallum, J Kelly, J McLaren, John Coleman.

Celtic is recognised as one the game's great institutions, yet the club had the most humble of beginnings. It was founded in 1887 by a group of gentlemen who knew little about football but a lot about need and wanted to raise money to help the Catholic poor of the East End of Glasgow. One of the prime movers was Brother Walfrid. Born within a fortnight of the Penny Black's introduction in May 1840 in the sleepy County Sligo village of Ballymote as Andrew Kerins, he joined the Marists Priests Teaching Order in 1864 and subsequently settled in Glasgow's East End. He taught in St Mary's and later became headmaster of the newly opened Sacred Heart School, but also found the time to run youth football teams and organise exhibition games for charity. Noting the success of Hibs in Auld Reekie, the representatives of St Mary's, St Andrew's and St Alphonsus' parishes decided it was time Glasgow had its own Irish football club. Brother Walfrid advocated the name 'Celtic' . . . the rest is history.

The team's soccer baptism was an Old Firm battle on May 28th 1888, won handsomely by five goals to two. Do you think Rangers muttered to themselves about beginners' luck . . . ?

THE EARLY YEARS

By 1889, the team's second season, Celtic had already become a team to contend with and reached the Scottish Cup Final which they lost 2-1 to Third Lanark Rifle Volunteers. In 1967, the year Celtic were crowned kings of Europe, the Hi-Hi's slipped out of existence.

Celtic's first Scottish Cup win came in 1892, when they drubbed Queen's Park 5-1 in the final. The following year they finished top of the League for the first time, stealing the title by a point from their Old Firm rivals.

One of the great factors behind Celtic's success has to be continuity. On that famous night of 25 May 1967, Jock Stein was only the fourth manager of the club since its beginnings, seventy-nine years before. Celtic's first manager was Willie Maley (pictured right), a brusque individual who also played in the club's first match. Maley and James Kelly, Celtic's first captain and later Chairman, were the club's early visionaries. They introduced floodlights, even before the turn of the century, for the 1893 Christmas Day match with Clyde.

Little is available to the collector for Celtic's first ten years. J Baines of Bradford and Barnsley sold cards in packets though from 1880 until 1920. These delightful cards are reproduced here actual size (the packet has been reduced in size so we could illustrate more of the cards). They came in shapes such as diamonds, hearts, rectangles, fans and balls and were usually full colour. Some name a player, others just have a simple caption. All are rare. About a dozen different Celtic cards are known to exist. Pears Soap gave away similar cards – they are even rarer.

The 1896 team
Back row: T Maguire (Trainer), J Kelly, Alan Martin, D Doyle, B Battles, W Ferguson.
Middle row: J Madden, A McMahon, P Meechan, W Maley
Front row: J Blessington, the Glasgow Cup, D McArthur.

It was crisis on and off the field during the 1896-97 season. Dissatisfaction with press reports led to three players going on strike before a league game against Hibs and what was probably Celtic's worst ever result occurred shortly afterwards – a 4-2 defeat by Arthurlie in the first round of the Scottish Cup.

Three Nuns Tobacco seems an unlikely name for a brand of the weed. Perhaps that's why the set of 30 'Footballers' given out by manufacturers J & F Bell are so extremely rare. The card has been enlarged from its actual size here; the text on the reverse informs that the 5' 10" Bernard (Barney) Battles was born in Springburn, a versatile defender signed by Celtic in 1895, who had previously played for Hearts.

The 1897 squad
Back row: J Curran, D McArthur, J Blessington, J Cullen, T Bonnar (Trainer), T Dunbar, J Campbell, J Reynolds, P Gallacher
Middle row: Joe Cassidy, J Madden, J Kelly, D Doyle, W Maley
Front row: J Divers, A McMahon, C McEleny

As the 1896-97 season came to a close Celtic's troubles continued. In spite of reaching the Glasgow Cup Final they lost 3-1 to their bitter rivals from across the city in the replay. They were losing out to professionalism and it was only by changing from charitable status and becoming a limited company in March 1897 that team building proper could begin again.

The 1898 squad
Back row: D Friel (Trainer), R Davidson, Alex King, W Maley (Manager), Willie Orr, John Hodge, Tom Hynds
Middle row (seated): D Storrier, B Battles, H Goldie, J Welford, D Doyle, J Campbell, A McMahon, P Gilhooly
Front row: J Fisher, Dan McArthur, Jack Bell

Willie Maley, flush with the newly-raised capital, signed up Willie Orr and John Campbell, who previously had left Celtic due to, as Maley put it, 'the stupid action of a very prominent committee man'. This strengthened team cruised to a League Championship win without a single defeat, and with only three draws out of a total of eighteen matches.

R. FINDLAY,
Glasgow Celtic.

A. KING,
Glasgow Celtic.

DAN DOYLE,
Glasgow Celtic.

GEO. LIVINGSTONE,
Glasgow Celtic.

B. BATTLES,
Glasgow Celtic.

W. ORR,
Glasgow Celtic.

A. McMAHON,
Glasgow Celtic.

F & J Smith, the Glasgow cigarette manufacturers who later became part of Imperial Tobacco, issued this set of 120 'Footballers' (usually known as 'Smith's Brown Backs') in early 1900. Sandy McMahon (shown left) – nicknamed 'Duke' was regarded as one of the great headers of the ball. Born in Selkirk, he played for Celtic from January 1891 until October 1903.

D. McARTHUR,
Glasgow Celtic.

J. CAMPBELL,
Glasgow Celtic.

The 1901 team with the Exhibition Cup.
Back row: B Battles, W Loney, H Marshall, J Moir, A McMahon, H Watson, John Campbell, W Orr, A McPherson, D McLeod, P Somers
Front row: J Quinn, J McMenemy, W McCaffrey, W Maley (Manager), A Crawford, T McDermott, D Hamilton.

This was the year Jimmy Quinn made his debut. He started off at outside-left and moved to centre-forward when David Hamilton arrived. But spectators in the old pavilion shown in the photo could be hard-pushed to see them – they had to continually wipe its condensation steamed-up windows during matches.

Ogdens issued these cards, known as 'Tabs', between 1899 and 1904. There are sports series and general interest series and some Celtic players are featured, although some like J Divers had, by the time his card appeared, moved on to Hibs.

Some players feature on more than one card and two of the general interest cards show the match in progress on the day of the 1902 Ibrox Disaster.

To my Football Enthusiast from 12/11/03.   J.McG.

This is a rare postcard (only one example seen by me over fifteen years) to commemorate the opening of New Hampden Park at Mount Florida, just south of the Old Hampden Park (which Third Lanark moved into).

This is an extremely rare German postcard showing Celtic playing a match in Leipzig in 1906.

The team lined up at the Leipzig game: Ned Garry, Don McLeod, Alex McNair, Jimmy Quinn, Peter Somers, Davie Adams, Willie Maley (Manager), James Young, Jimmy Hay, James Bauchop, David Hamilton, Bobby Templeton.

R. Davis, *Trainer*. R. G. Campbell. D. McLeod. H. Watson. D. Hamilton. A. McNair. A. Wilson. E. Garry. J. McCourt. D. Adams.
J. Young. J. Hay. A. Bennett. J. McMenemy. W. Loney. J. Quinn. P. Somers. W. McNair.
CELTIC FOOTBALL CLUB
Cup Tie and League Team, 1905-06.

Between 1905 and 1910 Celtic won six successive championships. The first, 1904-05 found Celtic tied on points with their auld enemy, but they won the play-off at Hampden 2-1. In the 1905-06 season they also took the Glasgow Cup beating Third Lanark 3-0 in the final.

14

A. Bennett, A. McNair, D. McLeod, J. Young, D. Adams, W. Orr, R. Templeton, J. Hay, R. Davis.
D. Hamilton, J. McMenemy, P. Somers, R Craig, J. Bauchop, W. Loney, J. Quinn, A. Wilson, E. Garry

CELTIC F.C., 1906-07

Goalkeeper Adams was injured in a pre-season Old Firm benefit match. Celtic's old rivals loaned them Tom Sinclair, who to his eternal credit was outstanding, letting only two goals past him in first class matches, these being in the 1906 Glasgow Cup Final when, ironically, Celtic won 3-2 against Sinclair's "own" team. After Adams returned Celtic went on to win the League.

COPE'S "CLIPS" CIGARETTES

No. 405.- HAMILTON, D. Celtic

Noted Footballers

COPE'S "CLIPS" CIGARETTES

No. 403.- JOHNSTONE, P. Celtic

Noted Footballers

COPE'S "CLIPS" CIGARETTES

No. 402.- MITCHELL, J. Celtic

Noted Footballers

NOTED FOOTBALLERS No 121.

HAMILTON, GLASGOW CELTIC.

COPE'S "Solace" CIGARETTE

NOTED FOOTBALLERS No 122.

WEIR. GLASGOW CELTIC

COPE'S "Solace" CIGARETTES.

COPE'S "CLIPS" CIGARETTES

No. 408.—LONEY, W. Celtic

Noted Footballers

COPE'S "CLIPS" CIGARETTES

No. 400.—McMENEMY Celtic

Noted Footballers

NOTED FOOTBALLERS No 123.

ADAMS, GLASGOW CELTIC

COPE'S "Solace" CIGARETTES

NOTED FOOTBALLERS No 124.

HAY, GLASGOW CELTIC

COPE'S "Solace" CIGARETTES

NOTED FOOTBALLERS No 125.

QUINN. GLASGOW CELTIC

COPE'S "Solace" CIGARETTES

Cope Brothers 'Noted Footballers Clips Cigarettes' from 1910 ; there are nine Celtic players in this very elusive set. The ones not illustrated are T McAteer (401), A McNair (404), J Quinn (406), J Dodds (407).

'Noted Footballers', given with 'Solace' Cigarettes, also in 1910 was a huge set of 195 cards. Above and on facing page are the Celtic cards – numbers 121 to 135.

LONIE.
GLASGOW CELTIC.

COPE'S "Solace" CIGARETTES

SOMERS,
GLASGOW CELTIC.

COPE'S "Solace" CIGARETTES

MacLEAN,
GLASGOW CELTIC.

COPE'S "Solace" CIGARETTES

McNAIR,
GLASGOW CELTIC.

COPE'S "Solace" CIGARETTES

MITCHELL,
GLASGOW CELTIC.

COPE'S "Solace" CIGARETTES

YOUNG,
GLASGOW CELTIC.

COPE'S "Solace" CIGARETTES.

MACMENEMY,
GLASGOW CELTIC.

COPE'S "Solace" CIGARETTES.

MacLEOD,
GLASGOW CELTIC.

COPE'S "Solace" CIGARETTES.

MORON,
GLASGOW CELTIC.

COPE'S "Solace" CIGARETTES.

KIVLICHAN,
GLASGOW CELTIC.

COPE'S "Solace" CIGARETTES

F & J Smith's 1908 'Footballers'. The set of 100 cards runs from 2 to 104 (numbers 1, 13, 53 and 54 were unissued). Six Celts are featured in the set. Other ex-Celts appear in the set – D Mcleod (Middlesborough) for example. This issue is often referred to as the 'Footballers Cup Tie ' set. On the left is a thin paper advert, probably an insert in a newspaper, found by a workman who uncovered it behind an old fireplace.

T. McMENEMY
CELTIC F.C.

J. QUINN
CELTIC F.C.

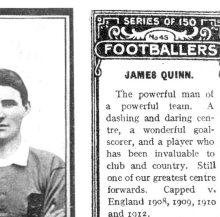

SERIES OF 150
No 45
FOOTBALLERS

JAMES QUINN.

The powerful man of a powerful team. A dashing and daring centre, a wonderful goal-scorer, and a player who has been invaluable to club and country. Still one of our greatest centre forwards. Capped v. England 1908, 1909, 1910 and 1912.

SMITH'S
GLASGOW MIXTURE
CIGARETTES

A. McNAIR
CELTIC F.C.

P. GALLAGHER
CELTIC F.C.

J. DODDS
CELTIC F.C.

'Footballers' – a series of 150 issued in 1912. Several printings were made and the backs of these cards can be found in various shades of blue or black. The text can occasionally vary and there are minor design changes between printings too, with keylines appearing or disappearing.

J. YOUNG
CELTIC F.C.

INTERNATIONAL FOOTBALL MATCH : Scotland v. England, Hampden Park, Glasgow, April 2, 1910.

Three Celts – Hay, McMenemy and Quinn, together with an ex-Celt Bennett helped Scotland to win 2-0 in front of a crowd of 110,000. The goals came in the first half, from McMenemy and Quinn. The latter's goal was typical of the strong, robust man who bundled ball and keeper into the net.

T. SINCLAIR.

CELTIC'S RECORD.
CELTIC, 6; MOTHERWELL, 0 (League)
CELTIC, 5; KILMARNOCK, 0 (League)
CELTIC, 2; CLYDE, 0 · · · (League)
CELTIC, 2; MORTON, 0 · · · (League)
CELTIC, 2; PARTICK THISTLE 0 (G.C.)
CELTIC, 3; HEARTS, 0 · · · (League)
CELTIC, 5 QUEEN'S PARK, 0 · (G.C.)
CELTIC, 2; THIRD LANARK 0 (League)
CELTIC, 2; AIRDRIEONIANS 0 (League)

Star Billiard Rooms. 483 New City Road, Glasgow,
T. SINCLAIR. Proprietor.

Left: Tom Sinclair, the Rangers player who turned in such a fine performance for Celtic (see page 15), went on to own the Star Billiard Rooms after his retirement from the game, but as this rare postcard shows, had no qualms about immodestly exploiting the novelty value of his crossing the tracks in the interests of promoting his business.

Right: By contrast Jimmy Quinn was clearly still playing when this card was published.

Maclure, Macdonald & Co.   *Copyright.*

JAMES QUINN, CELTIC F.C.

Celtic

Neither tripping, kicking nor jumping at a player shall be allowed. A player shall not use his hands to hold or push his opponent, or play in any manner likely to cause injury.

GALLAHER'S CIGARETTES.

JAMES HAY,
GLASGOW CELTIC, 1909-10.

A few odd rare Celtic cards from various sets of the period –

far left: Anonymously published plain-backed 'Football Teams and Rules', circa 1910.

left: 'Association Football Club Colours', no. 78 of a set of 100, 1910.

right: William Angus, on Celtic books before the War and awarded the VC for his rescue of a senior officer, commemorated on no. 79 of Cohen Weenen & Co.'s 1916 set of cigarette cards 'VC Heroes'. Due to his injuries he was unable to play again, but continued to be employed at Parkhead as a steward.

'International Footballers, 1909-10', an unnumbered set, shows the players involved in the Home International Championships of that season. Also featured in this 1910 set are A Bennett and J Hay.

Lance-Corpl WM. ANGUS.

A. MC. NAIR (Half Back)
SCOTLAND.

J. MC. MENEMY (Forward)
SCOTLAND.

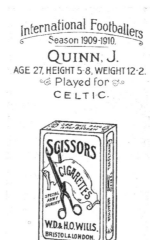

International Footballers
Season 1909-1910.
QUINN, J.
AGE 27, HEIGHT 5-8, WEIGHT 12-2.
Played for
CELTIC.

SCISSORS
CIGARETTES
SPECIAL ARMY QUALITY
W.D. & H.O. WILLS.
BRISTOL & LONDON.

W. LONEY (Half Back)
SCOTLAND.

J. QUINN (Forward)
SCOTLAND.

Back Row: D HAMILTON, D. MUNRO, J MCMENEMY, J. MITCHELL, W. KIVLICHAN.
Middle Row: P. JOHNSTONE, JAS. YOUNG, J. HAY, P. SOMERS, J. QUINN, A MCNAIR, D ADAMS, JAS. MCINTOSH, R. DAVIES *(TRAINER)*
Front Row: W. GLOVER, JOHN YOUNG, D. MCLEAN, L. MCLEAN, JAS. DODDS, W. LONEY, JAS. WEIR.

I have 15 postcards of different Scottish teams, given out by the magazine *Ideas* circa 1910. The missing one is suspected to be Queen's Park, but I would be delighted to hear from any reader who can help me complete my collection.

W. QUINN *Trainer*,   W. LONEY,   J. MCMENEMY,   J DODDS,   J. QUINN,   P. JOHNSTONE,   MR. W. MALEY, *Secy*.
J. BROWN,   A. MCATEE,   T MCGREGOR,   J. YOUNG,   P. GALLAGHER,   J. MULROONEY,   A. MCNAIR

Shaw, McNair and Dodds formed an iron defence that allowed Celtic to win the championship four times in a row between 1914 and 1917. This picture has been slightly reduced to fit the page size; the original A4 size coloured card is believed to have been a give-away with one of the many Glasgow weekly papers of the time.

A. McATEE,
Celtic F.C.

P. GALLACHER,
Celtic F.C.

JOE DODDS,
Celtic F.C.

JAMES QUINN,
Celtic F.C.

P. JOHNSTONE,
Celtic F.C.

The *Glasgow Weekly Mail* 'Series of Famous Footballers' of 1913-14, sheets of nine head and shoulder portraits, presumably a sheet given away with each issue over eleven weeks. Each sheet featured a different position such as 'Scotland's Favourite Goalkeepers' or 'Scotland's Favourite Right Backs' etc. Neither the 'Outside Lefts' nor the 'Centre Half Backs' include any Celtic players. Missing here, from the 'Right Backs' page, is Alex McNair.

J. McMENEMY,
Celtic F.C.

CHAS. SHAW,
Celtic F.C.

J. YOUNG,
Celtic F.C.

CELTIC F.C.
League Champions and Winners of the Scottish Cup, 1913-14.

BACK ROW: W MALEY (MANAGER), McMASTER, DODDS, SHAW, McNAIR, JOHNSTONE, McCOLL, QUIN (TRAINER)
FRONT ROW: McATEE, GALLAGHER, YOUNG (CAPT.), McMENEMY, BROWNING

This postcard shows the team at the start of their four-in-a-row championship run. In this season they also won the Scottish Cup, trouncing Hibs 4-1, and the Glasgow Charity Cup when they destroyed Third Lanark amidst a riot of goals. Dodds, McColl, McMaster, Johnstone and McMenemy (2) were the scorers in this 6-0 rout. McColl was by this time regarded as the 'new Jimmy Quinn' and went on to score 123 goals in 169 games.

OUR FOOTBALL BOYS No. 3.

ALEC McNAIR (Celtic). A household word in Glasgow. Plays right-back, stands 5 ft. 8 ins., weighs 11 st. 10 lbs., has lots of caps, and comes from Stenhousemuir.

F. & J. SMITH'S CIGARETTES

CELTIC.
A. McNAIR.

FOOTBALL CLUB RECORDS.
A SERIES OF 50.—No. 6

CELTIC.
(CHAMPIONS.)

SCOTTISH LEAGUE, RECORD 1921-2.

	Home.	Away.
Aberdeen	w 2—0	D 1—1
Airdrieonians	w 1—0	w 2—0
Albion Rovers	w 3—1	w 2—0
Ayr United	w 2—1	D 0—0
Clyde	w 1—0	D 1—1
Clydebank	w 6—0	w 2—0
Dumbarton	w 4—0	w 5—0
Dundee	w 4—0	D 0—0
Edin. Hibernians	w 3—1	L 1—2
Falkirk	D 0—0	D 1—1
Glasgow Rangers	D 0—0	D 1—1
Greenock Morton	w 1—0	D 1—1
Hamilton Acads.	w 4—0	w 3—1
H. of Midlothian	w 3—0	w 2—1
Kilmarnock	w 1—0	L 3—4
Motherwell	w 2—0	D 1—1
Partick Thistle	w 3—0	D 0—0
Queen's Park	w 3—1	w 3—1
Raith Rovers	w 4—0	D 1—1
St. Mirren	w 2—0	w 2—0
Third Lanark	w 2—0	D 0—0

Total played, 42; W., 27; L., 2; D., 13. Goals for, 83 ; against, 20. Points, 67.

Issued by The Imperial Tobacco Co. (of Great Britain & Ireland), Limited.

F. & J. SMITH'S CIGARETTES

CELTIC.
A. McNAIR.

In Maley's *The Story of Celtic* book McNair is one of twelve players singled out for special mention. This outstanding defender joined the Celts in 1904 from Stenhousemuir and for twenty years the calm, intelligent player served Celtic well. The postcard on the left is no. 3 from a set of twelve. The F & J Smith cigarette cards are from two similar sets of 'Football Club Records' issued in 1917 and 1922. Both featured McNair, although he has more hair on the earlier card. McNair also features on no. 45 of Churchman's 'Footballers', coloured action pictures with a sepia portrait inset.

CHURCHMAN'S CIGARETTES

A. McNAIR.

W. CRINGAN.
Plays centre-half for Celtic. Scottish International.

Willie Cringan, born in Muirkirk, signed for Sunderland in 1910 and went on to become a brilliant caption of Celtic. He guested for the team while still serving in the Army and eventually was signed in 1917 for six hundred pounds. He was also a superb quoits player and was the Scottish Champion in 1926.

Left: A postcard size card (reduced here), one of a set of ten Scottish footballers issued by the periodical, *The Nelson Lee Library*.
Right: Godfrey Phillips issued this card in three sizes.
Below ,far left and far right: The *Magnet Library* gave this series of 'Footballers' cards away with the comic each week, some as singles and some as pairs.
Below ,second from right: 'Sport and Adventure' July 29 1922.
Below, second from left and centre: Front and back of card given with *Boys' Magazine* from 1922 to 1923. Only eight of the 'Coloured Studies of Famous Internationals' were issued, and Cringan the only Scot amongst them.

W. CRINGAN

390   CELTIC

WILLIAM CRINGAN

W. CRINGAN (Glasgow Celtic)

"BOYS' MAGAZINE"
Coloured Studies of
Famous Internationals

W. CRINGAN

(Glasgow Celtic)

A brilliant centre half-back who has played for Scotland. He was once a member of Sunderland. Weighs 11 st. 6 lbs. and stands 5 ft. 8 ins.

Another Coloured Study Next Week.

Presented Free with
THE "MAGNET" LIBRARY
JUNE 3RD, 1922.
No. 7.
WILLIAM CRINGAN
Glasgow Celtic & Scottish International centre-half, who at one time played for Sunderland.

A splendid Real Photo of a famous footballer *in action* will be given Free with next Monday's "Magnet."

Back Row—W. Cringan, A. Longmuir, J. McMaster, P. Gallagher, J McFarlane, W. McStay, J. Gilchrist.
Middle Row— W. Quinn (Trainer), A. McNair, T. Craig, D. Livingstone, W. Lawrie, J Murphy, J. McKay, C. Watson.
Front Row— D. Pratt, T. McInally, A. McAtee, H. Brown, C. Shaw, J. Price, J. Cassidy, A McLean, Mr. W. Maley (Manager).

CELTIC FOOTBALL CLUB, 1920-1921.

This was not a great season for Celtic, runners-up in the league and put out of the Scottish Cup by Hearts. However, a 1-0 defeat of Clyde secured the Glasgow Cup and Tommy McInally's two goals against Rangers the Glasgow Charity Cup in the final at Hampden.

W. McSTEY

W. McSTAY

Gallaher's Cigarettes.

WM. McSTAY
GLASGOW CELTIC

PLAY UP CELTIC

This Netherburn born player, one of the greatest backs ever, came to Celtic at the age of 19 from Larkhall Thistle, immediately going on loan to Ayr United before returning for his league debut at Love Street on 19 August 1914, a 5-1 victory. His brother John was also a Celtic player and the family connection continues to the present day; the two brothers were the great-uncles of Paul McStay. William made nearly 500 appearances for Celtic, winning four League Championships, three Scottish Cup medals, besides also being capped thirteen times for Scotland. During his twenty year career he spent a short time in American soccer, returning in 1923 before being transferred to Hearts in 1929 to finish his playing career there. In 1932 he became manager of the Northern Ireland side Glentoran. One of the greats, he passed away in 1960.

Above, left: Pinnace, *Above, middle:* Adventure (front and back), *Above, right:* Gallaher's 'Footballers' *Right:* Champion 'Famous Footer Internationals'
Left: Boys Magazine 'Famous Footer Clubs'

W.McStay

CELTIC FOOTBALL CLUB, 1921-2

Ground: Celtic Park, Glasgow.   Colours: Green and white.

Left to right (back row): J. Connor, D. Pratt, J. M'Knight, C. Shaw, J. Cassidy (*S).   Middle row: W. Quinn (trainer), H. Hilley, A. M'Nair (*S), J. M'Stay, J. Dodds (*S), W. M'Stay (*S), T. M'Inally, S. Glasgow, J. Gilchrist.   Front row: J. Macfarlane, F. Collins, J. M'Master, A. M'Atee (*S), J. M'Kay, P. Gallacher, J. Murphy, A. M'Lean, W. Cringan (*S), W. Maley (manager).

Players starred are Internationals.   Photo by Agnew, Glasgow.

This insert was given away free in the *All Sports* magazine of 5 November 1921. What a squad of players! What would their market value be in the current transfer climate?

J. McFARLANE   A. McLEAN   P. CONNELLY   J. McMASTER   JOHN GILCHRIST   CELTIC

This series were produced by Godfrey Phillips Ltd. in the early 1920s and are better known as 'Pinnace' (a word sometimes used in the address on the backs of the cards). There are 2,462 cards and each comes in three sizes! Similar looking and numbered cards can be found with up to four different back designs and completing a set represents a considerable challenge, if not a lifetime's work!

The cards are shown actual size on this and the facing page. On this page are the Large size, but the largest size, on the right of the opposite page, was the Cabinet size (the Cabinet was a Victorian photo size obsolete by the 1920s), and these cards come as plain back only. Also on the opposite page, the smallest cards, the Miniature size. 25 Miniature or five Large could be exchanged for one Cabinet, and 100 Miniatures or 20 Large could be exchanged for a 'Large Real Photo of any of the League Teams'. This was a lot of cards to swap for one and maybe explains why the Celtic team photo has never been seen – unless of course you know otherwise. . . .

P. GALLAGHER
181 CELTIC

J. CAIRNEY
2025 CELTIC

JOHN GILCHRIST
83 CELTIC

Altogether sixteen Celtic stars are featured in the Pinnace sets. Stars not shown here include Alec McNair, W Cringan, W McStay, H Hilley, J Cassidy and J Murphy. Incidentally, a lot of confusion exists over how Patsy Gallagher's name is or was spelt, apparently arising from a misspelt nameplate on his door, but just for the record on his birth certificate it is spelt with a g.

TOM McINALLY
182 CELTIC

C. SHAW
391 CELTIC

1125   A. McATEE

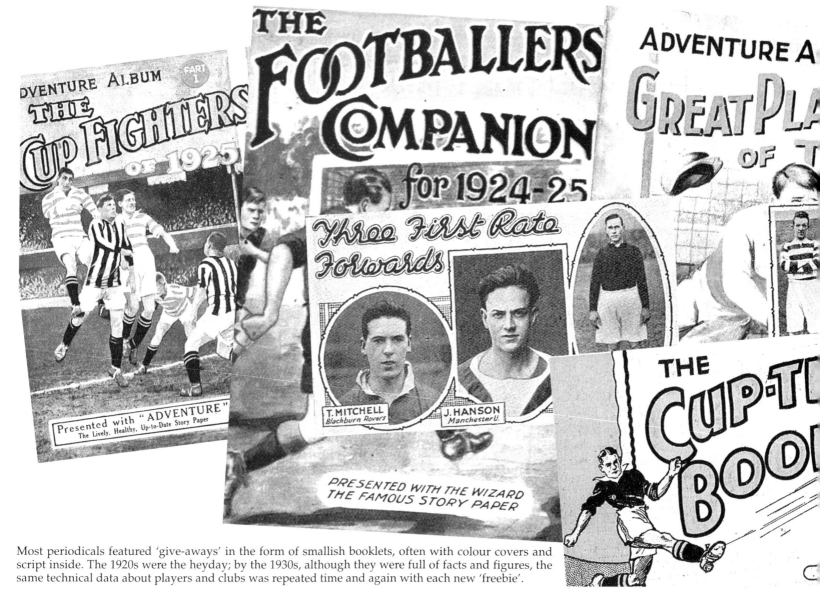

Most periodicals featured 'give-aways' in the form of smallish booklets, often with colour covers and script inside. The 1920s were the heyday; by the 1930s, although they were full of facts and figures, the same technical data about players and clubs was repeated time and again with each new 'freebie'.

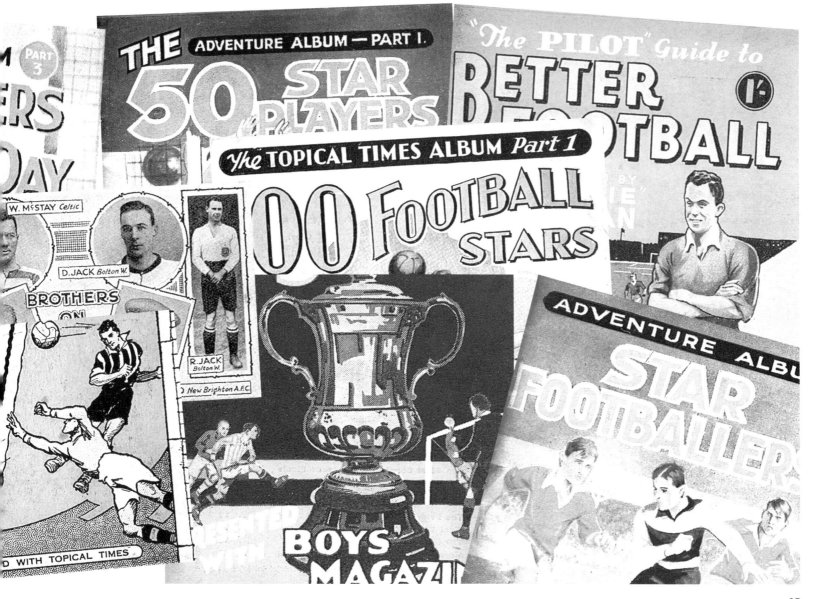

JAMES DELANEY.   Topical
Celtic F.C.   Times.

J. KENNAWAY

DELANEY

Some famous sons – Patsy Gallagher, a product of Clydebank Juniors, gained a big reputation as a player who worked tirelessly and skilfully, striking fear into the strongest defences. Joining Celts in 1911, he scored 196 goals and played in over 450 games. Jimmy Delaney, though small in stature, could score against the heaviest defences and is one of the Celtic Greats. Kennaway, one of the best goalies of the 1930s was much in demand, so much so that he was capped by two different countries. Canadian by birth, he played for that country against the USA, and by descent for Scotland.

J. DELANEY (CELTIC)

WILLS'S CIGARETTES

THIS SURFACE IS ADHESIVE ASK YOUR
TOBACCONIST FOR THE ATTRACTIVE
ALBUM (PRICE ONE PENNY) SPECIALLY
PREPARED TO HOLD THE COMPLETE SERIES

ASSOCIATION FOOTBALLERS
A SERIES OF 50

15
J. DELANEY
(Celtic)

A fast outside-right with a goal-scoring flair, James Delaney is a player with the big match temperament and he has been extremely successful in representative games. Born in Cleland, Lanarkshire, he learnt the game with the local club and joined Celtic in season 1933/34. He made his first appearance in the League team in the following season and after a short time made outside-right his own place. Delaney, appeared against England in the King George V Jubilee Trust Fund Match in 1935, and has since played against all the home countries as well as against Germany, Austria and Czechoslovakia.

W.D. & H.O. WILLS
MANUFACTURERS OF GOLD FLAKE, CAPSTAN,
WOODBINE AND STAR CIGARETTES
BRANCH OF THE IMPERIAL TOBACCO CO.
(OF GREAT BRITAIN & IRELAND), LTD.

J. DELANEY

P. GALLAGHER
CELTIC

M'INALLY
No. 4.
FOOTBALL
FREE
This Card is one of
a series of 15 Cards
Numbered 1 to 15.

JOE CASSIDY.
CELTIC.

Top left: Barratts (sweetie cigarettes) issued vast numbers of football cards. This one is Football Team Folders 'Scottish League – Division 1' season 1934-35.

Top middle: A very rare *Topical Times* metal issue 'Star Footballers' R Thomson.

Top right: Another metal *Topical Times* 'card', this one from 1931.

Far left and right: Two very rare cards from W & J McLintock of Glasgow, confectionery manufacturers. The offer of a free football in exchange for 15 cards was perhaps just too tempting and probably explains why these are now so hard to find.

Middle left: From an unnumbered set of 24 issued in 1924 by John Filshill of Glasgow and given away with 'Lotus' toffee.

Middle right: Maynards Confectionery 'Football Clubs' 1933.

M'LEAN
No. 8.
FOOTBALL
FREE
This Card is one of
a series of 15 Cards
Numbered 1 to 15.

See conditions other side.
[Over.

37

Many boys' comics gave away cards in the 1920s and 1930s. Illustrated here are just a few of the abundance of cards that can be collected. The card of Gilchrist is from a set of 'Sporting Champions' given away with *The Champion* (Amalgamated Press), 1922. Cassidy and T McInally (top) were free with the *Adventure* in 1923 as were the two little cards in the centre in 1934 – 'Footballers – Hunt the Cup Cards' (set of 52) and 'Football Team Cards' (set of 64). The little card of A McInally is from a D.C. Thomson set of 137 Footballers (mostly Scottish) issued in 1923. The other small cards were published by the *Nelson Lee Library*.

This Photograph is Presented FREE by WM. McEWAN & CO. Ltd.

CELTIC F·C

Back Row (*Left to Right*)—J. M'Menemy, P. Wilson, J. M'Farlane, J. M'Stay, P. Connelly.
Front Row (*Left to Right*)—M'Gonnigle, A. Thomson, W. M'Stay, J. M'Grory, Gray, J. Thomson

"PALS" NEW FOOTBALL SERIES

CELTIC F.C.

Back Row: H. Hilley, W. M'Stey, P. Gallacher, J. Gilchrist, J. Murphy.
Middle Row: J. M'Master, A. M'Nair, J. M'Farlane, S. Glasgow, A. M'Lean,
W. Cringan. Front Row: A. M'Atee, J. M'Stey, J. Murphy, C. Shaw, J. Cassidy,
W. Crilly, P. Connelly.

The Wm. McEwan card comes from a booklet of six postcards. The date of issue is believed to be around 1928, but nothing is known of how these cards were distributed – can anyone help with this information? The *Pals* card is printed in sepia-gravure and its back is plain. This elusive card was given away with the comic in 1923. The *Chums* card (both front and back illustrated) dates from 1922 and is one of a set of twenty.

GLASGOW CELTIC F.C., 1928

BACK ROW : P. Wilson, J. McGrory, W. McStay, J. Thomson, J. McMenemy, J. Macfarlane, E. McGarvie (Trainer).
FRONT ROW : T. McInally, P. Connolly, A. Thomson, A. McLean, J. Donoghue, J. McStay, H. Hilley.

This is a thin sepiagravure insert given out with this popular comic. 1928-29 saw McGrory out of action for much of the time and all in all this was not one of the club's best seasons. On 29 March 1929 fire destroyed the pavilion at Parkhead and the inferno consumed most of the club's records. For the rest of the season Celtic's home games were played elsewhere. Two of these, against Third Lanark and Falkirk, were played at Shawfield.

J. DELANEY   W. BUCHAN,   F. MURPHY.

This rare postcard shows three of Celtic's famous sons. Inside-right Willie Buchan joined Celts in 1932 after being spotted with Grange Rovers. He and Delaney formed the best partnership on the right wing in Scotland at the time. Outside-left Frank Murphy came from St Roch's and made his Celtic debut in 1934. He was a Scottish Junior Internationalist against Ireland that year also and in 1938 gained a full cap, against Holland.

In Loving Memory of
John Thomson,
accidentally killed at Ibrox Park 5th Sept. 1931
from The Board, Officials and Players
of the Celtic Football Club.

'They never die who live in the
hearts of those they leave behind'

Memorial to late J. Thomson at Celtic Park

J. THOMSON CELTIC

J. THOMSON

John Thomson 1909-1931

Born in Buckhaven on the 28th January 1909 to a mining family, he went down the pits when he was only fourteen. His footballing career began with a local Juvenile team ,Bowhill Rovers, from which he moved to Wellesley Juniors. It was there that Celtic's Chief Scout, Steve Callaghan, spotted him and for a £10 signing-on fee John Thomson became a Celtic player, the form being signed against a telegraph pole.

Thomson helped Celtic to win the Scottish Cup in 1927 and 1931. On 5 September 1931 he was making his 211th Celtic appearance, playing alongside his team-mates Cook, McGonagle, Wilson, McStay, Geatons, R Thomson, Scarff, A Thomson, McGrory and Napier, when tragedy struck. Only five minutes into the second half he was stretchered off after a collision with Rangers' Sam English.

John Thomson never regained consciousness and died shortly afterwards in the Victoria Infirmary. 30,000 people lined the route of his funeral and Willie Maley summed up their feelings in the words 'Of all the Great Celts that have passed over, he has an honoured place'.

After the collision, the game, which ended 0-0 continued, with Charlie Geatons taking over in goal. 'It was an accident' said Jimmy McGrory. Afterwards, macabre as it seems, postcards such as this were produced of the accident, but such is the public's morbid fascination.

W. McGONAGLE
CELTIC

W. McGONAGLE (CELTIC)

McGONAGLE
CELTIC.   SCOTLAND.

W. McGONAGLE

W. McGONAGLE

W. McGONAGLE

W. McGONAGLE
CELTIC

Left-back McGonagle trained as a motor mechanic and played with Duntocher Hibs before signing for Celtic and gaining his place in the team of 1927. He won Scottish Cup medals in 1931 and 1933. He returned to his home town of Hamilton in 1936 and started playing for the Accies like his father before him. (Another team close to my heart; my grandfather Thomas Marshall played for them before the Great War and my cousin James Low was with the Accies in the 1950s.)

W. McGONAGLE

© D.C. Thomson & Co. Ltd.

CELTIC F.C.— 1933-34
Back Row (left to right)— W. MALEY (Manager), A. THOMSON, R. HOGG, J. KENNAWAY, C. NAPIER, J. McGRORY, W. McGONAGLE
J QUSKLEY (Trainer), Front Row *(left to right)*—CRUM, C. GEATONS, J McSTAY, P. WILSON, H. O'DONNELL

A series of twenty British and foreign teams on large sheets of card, with two holes punched on one side, were given away with the *Sunday Post*. The idea of the punch-holes was so that the cards could be threaded with cord and then placed in the special album provided. Thanks are due to *The Sunday Post* for permission to reproduce this 1930s give-away.

CELTIC

Back Row (left to right)—Geatons, Hogg, Kennoway, M'Gonagle, M'Donald, and Paterson.

Front Row—Delaney, Buchan, O'Donnell (F.), Napier, and O'Donnell (H.).

This 1934-35 season photo comes from an album given free with the *Topical Times*. The O'Donnell brothers played from 1932-35 and helped to improve Celtic's fortunes. Hugh scored a hat-trick in the 1932-33 Scottish Cup match against Dunfermline. Celtic went on to win the final against Motherwell. Jimmy McGrory, who had replaced Frank O' Donnell, scored the only goal.

Give-away cards generally feature the first team and anything that features lesser mortals is extremely rare. This postcard size card (enlarged here) was given out by the club to record the achievement of the reserves. The back reads: ' The Celtic Football Club, Glasgow. Winners of Scottish 2nd XI Cup, 1934-35' the players are also listed:

Back row: W Maley (Manager), M McDonald, D Clancy, J Boyle, J Foley, W Fagan, W Hughes, W Quinn (Trainer)
Front row: J Delaney, J McInally, J Morrison, J Crum, W Dunn, J Fitzsimmons

WILLIAM BUCHAN.
Celtic F.C.

Topical
Times

C. NAPIER,
Celtic F.C.

TOPICAL
TIMES.

MALCOLM M'DONALD.
Celtic F.C.

TOPICAL
TIMES

FRANK MURPHY
Celtic F.C.

Topical
Times

During the 1930s the *Topical Times* gave away various sets of football cards. These come in various shapes and sizes, although five main sizes exist, with the largest an impressive 20 cm x 25 cm.

MITCHELL'S CIGARETTES   MITCHELL'S CIGARETTES   MITCHELL'S CIGARETTES   MITCHELL'S CIGARETTES   MITCHELL'S CIGARETTES

J. McSTAY
(CELTIC)

J. KENNAWAY
(CELTIC)

J. DELANEY (CELTIC)

W. LYON (CELTIC)

R. HOGG (CELTIC)

THIS SURFACE IS ADHESIVE. ASK YOUR
TOBACCONIST FOR THE ATTRACTIVE
ALBUM (PRICE ONE PENNY) SPECIALLY
PREPARED TO HOLD THE COMPLETE SERIES

SCOTTISH FOOTBALLERS

A SERIES OF 50

30

J. McSTAY

(Celtic)

A great club captain who radiates inspiration to his playing colleagues, James McStay moves about unostentatiously, always turning up at the right encouraging spot, whether in attack or defence. He has preserved the centre stem of Celts' transitional team with the late John Thomson in goal and McGrory at centre-forward. Although one of those exceptional players who does much better in club than representative football, he has gained a share of international honours. He has skippered several Cup-winning sides and has a breastful of League medals. McStay came from Larkhall Thistle and Celts first broke him in as a wing-half.

ISSUED BY

STEPHEN MITCHELL & SON

BRANCH OF THE IMPERIAL TOBACCO CO.
(OF GREAT BRITAIN & IRELAND), LTD.

Stephen Mitchell, the Glasgow cigarette manufacturer (and benefactor of the Mitchell Library), produced two football sets of 50 cards each. The first, in 1934, called 'Scottish Footballers', included four Celts (these are the head and shoulder portraits on this page). In 1935 a set entitled 'Scottish Football Snaps', showing action shots, was produced. Amongst the three featured Celtic players was Delaney, making a name for himself as being fast, tricky and not inclined to waste time in front of the goal.

THIS SURFACE IS ADHESIVE. ASK YOUR
TOBACCONIST FOR THE ATTRACTIVE
ALBUM (PRICE ONE PENNY) SPECIALLY
PREPARED TO HOLD THE COMPLETE SERIES

SCOTTISH FOOTBALL SNAPS

A SERIES OF 50

18

R. HOGG

(Celtic)

Celtic have had many famous full backs in their time, but none giving better promise than Bobby Hogg, a young man with excellent physique and splendid power both in tackling and kicking. He has only been with Celtic since 1931—he was previously a junior with Larkhall Thistle—but he has been a League team regular ever since Cook went to Everton. In the past two years he has been on the fringe of international honours, and would have received them if it had not been for the consistency of Anderson, the Hearts right back. Hogg's time will come.

ISSUED BY

STEPHEN MITCHELL & SON

BRANCH OF THE IMPERIAL TOBACCO CO.
(OF GREAT BRITAIN & IRELAND), LTD.

GLASGOW CELTIC F.C.

In 1936 Ardath Tobacco Co. Ltd. issued a marathon set of 165 Scottish Football Teams.
By this time Celtic had been League Champions eighteen times. The team line-up above is:
Back row: R Hogg, W McGonagle, J Kennaway, C Geatons, W Lyon, G Paterson
Front row: J Delaney, W Buchan, J McGrory, M MacDonald, J Crum

This is another plain-backed postcard given out by the club itself. The caption on the back reads: The Celtic Football Club Glasgow Winners of Scottish League, 1st Division Championship and Glasgow Charity Cup British Empire Exhibition Trophy 1937-38.
Standing: C Geatons, R Hogg, J Morrison, J Kennaway, G Paterson, J Carruth, J Divers
Sitting: W Maley, J Delaney, M MacDonald, W Lyon, J Crum, F Murphy, J McMenemy (Trainer)
A single goal in extra time was enough to give Celtic victory.

McGRORY
CELTIC.   SCOTLAND.

J. McGRORY.

MITCHELL'S CIGARETTES

J. McGRORY
CELTIC

J McGRORY

MITCHELL'S CIGARETTES

J. McGRORY

CARRERAS CIGARETTES

J. McGRORY
CELTIC

Born in 1904, Jimmy McGrory achieved his boyhood ambition when he signed for Celtic from St Roch's. After a distinguished playing career he went on to become manager of Kilmarnock and eventually, almost inevitably, returned to Parkhead as manager in 1945. In an amazing match on 14 Jan 1928 he scored eight out of nine goals against a hapless Dunfermline. This goal machine put 49 away in 1926-27 and a further 47 in 1927-28. Have a closer look at the card on the top left. Despite the caption, it's a horrible mistake by BDV Cigarettes – the player is actually McGrory (no relation) of Stoke City. When collecting, be careful!